To all the little explorers,
may you always remember to:

BE CURIOUS

BE CONFIDENT

BE KIND

BE YOU

CONTENTS

FACTFILE	01
MAP OF ZIMBABWE	03
INTRO	05
HELLO	07
WELCOME	09
MEET MY FAMILY	11
WHERE WE LIVE	13
LET'S EXPLORE	15
LET'S GO TO SCHOOL	27

LET'S PLAY	31
LET'S LEARN	33
LET'S SAY	37
LET'S EAT	39
LET'S CELEBRATE	41
LET'S GET LUCKY	47
LET'S DREAM	49
GOODBYE	53
FLAG	55
HISTORY	56

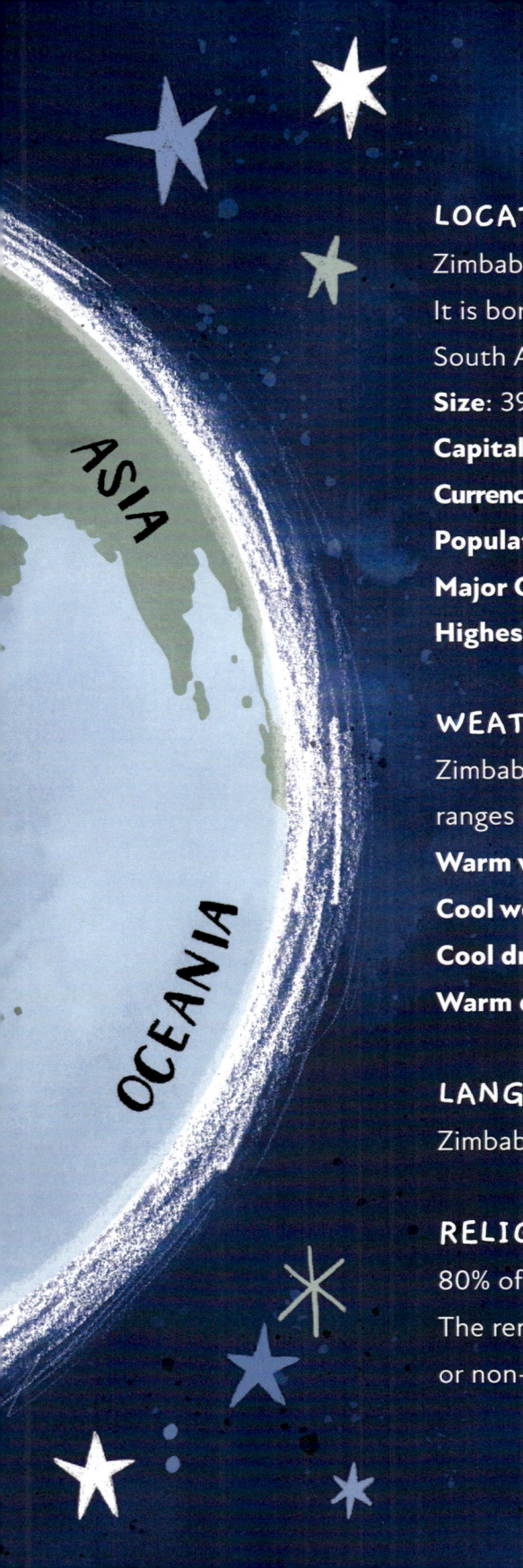

LOCATION

Zimbabwe is a country in Southern Africa. It is bordered by Zambia in the north, Mozambique in the east, South Africa in the south, and Botswana in the west.

Size: 390,757 km²
Capital: Harare 🔍
Currency: Zimbabwe dollar (ZWD) though US dollar (USD) is also used.
Population: 14.9 million (2020)
Major Cities: Harare, Bulawayo, Gweru, Chi Town (Chitungwiza) 🔍
Highest Point: Chimanimani Mountains at 2,592 m high

WEATHER

Zimbabwe has a subtropical climate where the temperature ranges between 6 and 33°C. There are four seasons:

Warm wet season: November-February
Cool wet season: March-April
Cool dry winter season: May-July
Warm dry season: August-October

LANGUAGES

Zimbabwe has 16 official languages.

RELIGION

80% of the population in Zimbabwe is Christian. The remaining population is Muslim, other faiths or non-religious.

★ INYANGANI

★ BVUMBA

★ CHIMANIMANI

KEEP AN EYE OUT FOR

Capital: Harare
Major Cities: Bulawayo, Gweru, Chi Town Mkoba
3 Mountains: Chimanimani, Bvumba, Inyangani
2 Rivers: Zambezi, Limpopo
Kariba Lake
The Big Tree
Hwange Park
Victoria Falls
Great Zimbabwe
Matopos

ARE YOU EXCITED ABOUT GOING ON AN ADVENTURE?

Join us on a journey across land and sea, taking you to Zimbabwe: the land of diamonds, platinum, and gold. It is a country filled with sensational scenery and wondrous wildlife. This book will guide you through the country's geography, people, culture, and beyond.

But there's more there than meets the eye: Zimbabwe has a great diversity of languages, communities, beliefs, and traditions. The people of Zimbabwe are known for being very warm, welcoming, and well-mannered, especially to their elders.

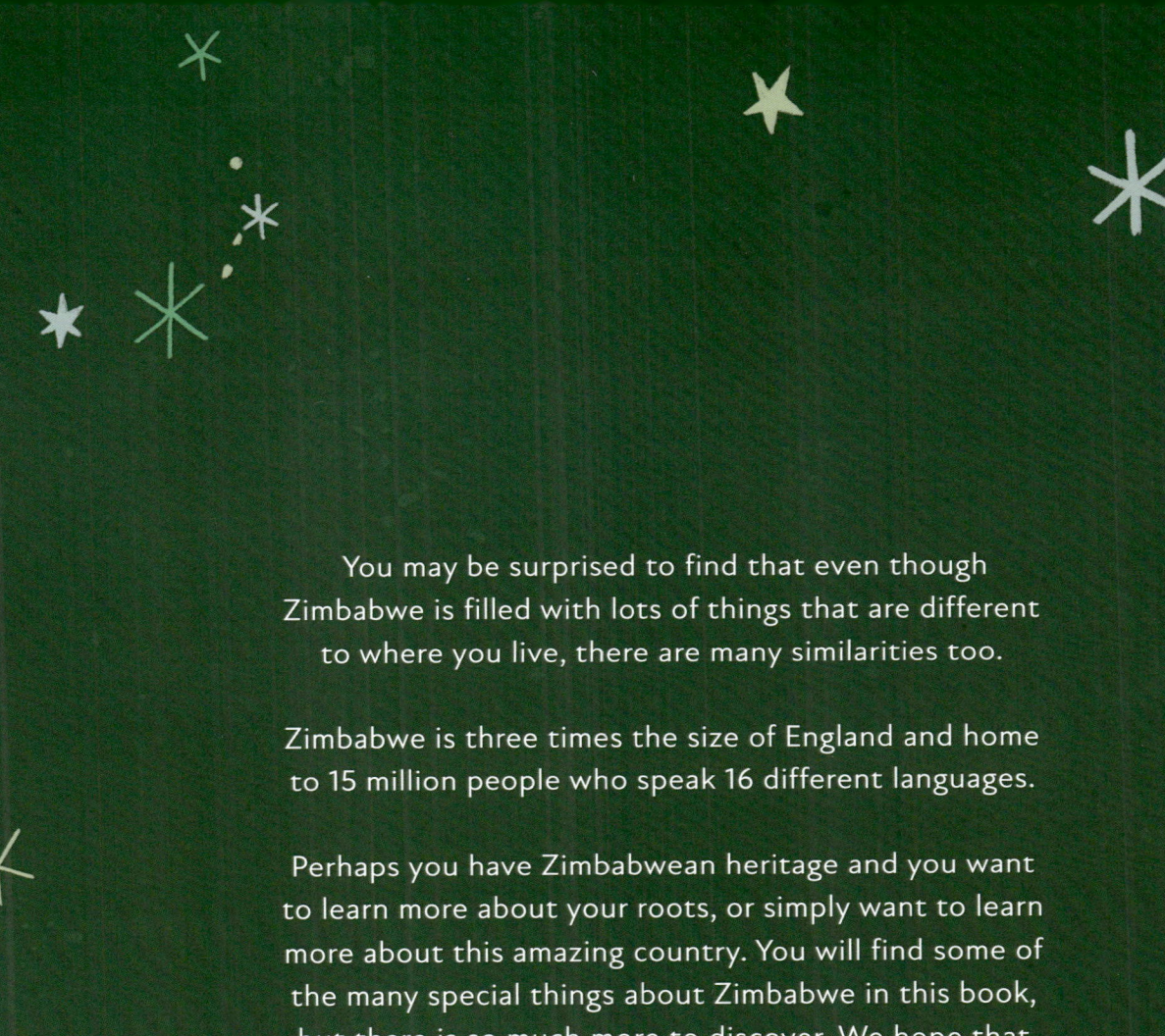

You may be surprised to find that even though Zimbabwe is filled with lots of things that are different to where you live, there are many similarities too.

Zimbabwe is three times the size of England and home to 15 million people who speak 16 different languages.

Perhaps you have Zimbabwean heritage and you want to learn more about your roots, or simply want to learn more about this amazing country. You will find some of the many special things about Zimbabwe in this book, but there is so much more to discover. We hope that you will be able to travel all the way to Zimbabwe and beyond someday.

THERE ARE 16 OFFICIAL LANGUAGES SPOKEN IN ZIMBABWE.

This is how to say 'hello' in six of them:

The other ten languages are: Tsonga, Kalanga, Khoisan, Nambya, Ndau, Chewa, Chibarwe, Shangaan, Tswana, and Venda.

LUMELA (SOUTHERN SOTHO)

HELLO

MHORO (SHONA)

Throughout the pages of this book you will find many words and phrases translated in:

Ndebele (red)
Shona (blue)

HI, WELCOME TO ZIMBABWE.
MY NAME IS TENDAI AND
I AM 9 YEARS OLD.

THIS IS MY YOUNGER BROTHER,
RANGARIRAI (RANGA FOR SHORT).
HE IS 6 YEARS OLD.

AND THIS IS MY BEST FRIEND,
MARVELOUS. HE IS THE
SAME AGE AS ME.

WE ARE REALLY EXCITED
TO SHOW YOU AROUND...
LET'S BEGIN OUR ADVENTURE!

MEET MY FAMILY

I live with Ranga, our baby sister Makawa, Mum, Dad, and our grandparents. We speak Shona and English. I have many aunts, uncles, and cousins too. Let me introduce you to my...

Family
Mhuri Imuli

Mum — Amai / Umama

Dad — Baba / Ubaba

Sister — Sisi / Udadewethu

Brother — Bhudi / Umfowethu

Auntie — Tete Mai / Ubabakazi

Uncle — Babamukuru / Umalume

Grandad — Sekuru / Ukhulu

Grandma — Ambuya / Ugogo

Cousin – there is no 'cousin' in Zimbabwean culture. Cousins are seen as brothers and sisters.

MARVELOUS' FAMILY LIVE NEXT DOOR.
They speak Ndebele and English.

'Ambuya' and 'Sekuru' aren't just the names for our own grandparents;
we call Marvelous' mum and dad and lots of other adults these names too.
My dad says that this is how we show our respect to those who are older than us.

DID YOU KNOW?

Many Zimbabweans have two names: a traditional name that usually has a meaning and an English name. My English name is Margaret and Ranga's is Keith. Marvelous also has a traditional name, which is Mandla. This is what our traditional names mean:

Tendai – Be thankful (in Shona)
Rangarirai – To remember (in Shona)
Mandla – Strength and power (in Ndebele)

Friend
Shamwari
Umngani

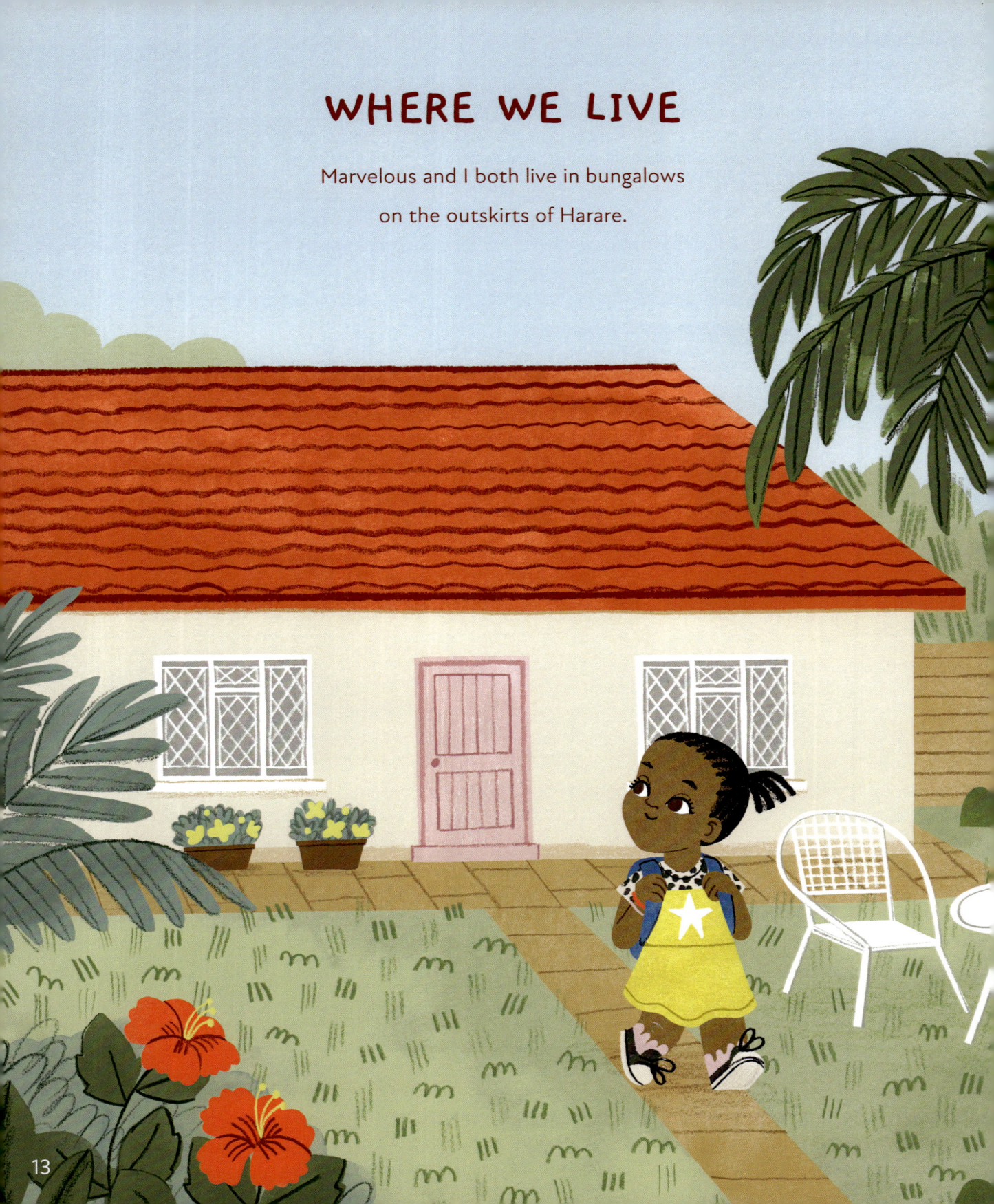

WHERE WE LIVE

Marvelous and I both live in bungalows on the outskirts of Harare.

My cousins, Fadzai and Rufaro, live in an apartment in Bulawayo.

Fadzai and Rufaro's home

Tete Mai Paul (Aunty Fadzai) lives in a small two-roomed house in Mkoba. 🔍

Tete Mai Paul's home

Home
Kumba
Ngekhaya

LET'S EXPLORE

LANDSCAPES

Ranga and I love visiting different parts of Zimbabwe to see the rest of our family. The view on the way is spectacular wherever we go. Sometimes Amai and Baba take the longer route, just so we can explore somewhere new. Here are some of the things we have seen along the way...

Explore
Ferefeta
Ukudinga

MOUNTAINS 🔍
There are 4,430 mountains in Zimbabwe; these are the three largest:

Chimanimani

Bvumba

Inyangani Mountains

RIVERS 🔍
There are 32 rivers in Zimbabwe but the 2 main ones are the Zambezi and the Limpopo.

The Zambezi is the fourth largest river in Africa. It flows through six different countries, starting in Zambia.

Q: How many elephants long is the Zambezi?
A: 375,342 elephants long – 2,740 km long

The Limpopo is smaller than the Zambezi. It flows through four countries, starting in South Africa.

Q: How many elephants long is the Limpopo?
A: 240,000 elephants long – 1,750 km long

Both rivers end in Mozambique where they flow into the Indian Ocean.

LAKES

There are six lakes in Zimbabwe, all of which are man-made. The biggest is Lake Kariba. It is great for fishing but not for swimming in, as you are likely to bump into a crocodile or two.

WATERFALLS

There are several waterfalls in Zimbabwe including Bridal Veil, Mtarazi, Nyangombe, and Nyamuziwa Falls. Many have long winding roads leading up to the top where you can see the beautiful views. If you are lucky, you can swim in the cold pools at the bottom. The largest and most famous waterfall is Victoria Falls.

SAVANNAS

These grasslands are flat, open spaces with trees, and the grass turns golden during the hot dry season. You can go on a safari there to see wild animals such as lions and giraffes.

EVERGREEN FOREST

These forests are full of trees that are green all year round (evergreen). There are many evergreen forests in the Eastern Highlands where it is often rainy and foggy.

DID YOU KNOW?

Zimbabwe is a landlocked country, which means you have to travel through another country to get to the seaside.

PLANTS AND TREES

There are thousands of different types of plants and trees in Zimbabwe. Ranga loves the snot apple, knobbly thorn, mohobohobo, and sausage trees because their names make him laugh.

My favourite is the upside-down tree. Its name is actually the baobab tree and its branches look like roots. Its fruit is called monkey bread. Ambuya used to climb baobab trees when she was little. Now when she goes shopping, she buys us yummy monkey bread – she says it is very good for us. She loves it because she says it keeps her looking young.

Tree
Muti
Isihlahla

FACTS:

The baobab can live for over 5,000 years. It can grow up to 30 m high and 50 m wide.

The baobab is also known as 'the tree of life'.

Their trunks can store over 100,000 litres of water, which allows them to grow fruit even when it doesn't rain for a long time. The baobab is used as shelter, food, and water for both animals and humans. During the dry season, elephants tear the bark to get water from the flesh inside the tree.

The most well-known baobab in Zimbabwe is called 'The Big Tree', which measures 22 m wide and 24 m tall. Some say it is around 1,500 years old.

DID YOU KNOW?

The baobab tree is not only famous around the world but also stars in movies. Have you spotted it in any of these films?

The Lion King
As Rafiki's (the monkey) tree

Madagascar
The largest tree on the island, which holds the plane that is the royal residence of King Julien XIII.

THE FLAME LILY

This is the national flower of Zimbabwe. It can grow up to 3 m high. Amai warns us to stay away from it as it is very poisonous. It can make your skin sore from just touching it *and* it can kill you if you eat it.

ANIMALS
Mhuka *Inyamazana*

When sisi Nyarie and bhudi Munyaradzi (our cousins from England) came to stay, we went on a trip to Hwange National Park. We were all so excited because we saw lions, buffalos, and elephants. These are three of what is known as 'The Big Five'. I hope that one day Ranga, Makawa, and I get to see leopards and rhinos too. 🔍

The Big 5 got their name because they are the top five animals that hunters used to want to catch the most. Nowadays these animals are the ones people most want to see:

African Lion
African Leopard
African Elephant
Cape Buffalo
Rhinoceros

HERE ARE SOME OF THE MANY OTHER ANIMALS AND INSECTS YOU MAY FIND IN ZIMBABWE – SEE IF YOU CAN SPOT THEM:

Zebra, giraffe, crocodile, zorille, hippopotamus, warthog, Roan antelope, African wild dog, pangolin, Samango monkey, black mamba snake, African fish eagle, emperor swallowtail butterfly.

DID YOU KNOW?

The Big Five animals can only be found together in thirteen countries in the world.

VICTORIA FALLS 🔍

Last summer, I visited Victoria Falls with Marvelous and his family. It is one of the greatest attractions in Africa, as well as one of the Seven Natural Wonders of the World. We call it Mosi-O-Tunya which means *'the smoke that thunders'* because the spray from the falling water rises 400m and can be seen and heard 40–50 km away.

DID YOU KNOW?

If you visit Victoria Falls at night, you might get lucky and see a moonbow in the sky above the Falls. A moonbow is the same as a rainbow but it is only seen at night because it is created by moonlight rather than sunlight.

GREAT ZIMBABWE RUINS 🔍

Great Zimbabwe is an ancient city that was built from stone almost 1,000 years ago. It took around 300 years to build.

MATOBO NATIONAL PARK 🔍 – THE MATOPOS

Marvelous and I also went on a school trip here, to Zimbabwe's oldest national park. There are lots of trees, plants, and animals, as well as the famous balancing rocks. These rocks are known as 'Mother and Child' because of the way they look.

LEGEND HAS IT...

...that Nyami Nyami (the river god) lived with his wife in the Zambezi River, but they were separated by a dam. When the dam was being built, there were the worst floods ever known, which knocked the dam down. Although they began rebuilding the dam the following year, there was an even worse flood, destroying the dam once again. Eventually the dam was completed in 1960. Whenever there are tremors, the Tonga people believe that Nyami Nyami is trying to reach his wife on the other side of the dam and one day he will again destroy it.

KARIBA DAM 🔍

The Kariba Dam on the Zambezi River is the largest man-made reservoir in the world. It was built to provide electricity to Zimbabwe and Zambia. Tete Mai Masimba (Aunty Kundai) loves to tell us the story of Nyami Nyami.

LET'S GO TO SCHOOL

Marvelous, Ranga, and I go to the same primary school in Harare. Marvelous and I are in third grade and Ranga is in first grade. Ranga started school this year.

School
Chikoro
Isikolo

Our school is big, with many classrooms. There are lots of fields where we run around and play sports. We learn in English but we also study Shona. Each day we catch the school bus to and from school.

Bhudi Panashe (our cousin) lives in the rural area of Makoba. His school is quite different to ours as it is much smaller with only one classroom. He says it can get very full when everyone tries to squeeze in. His lessons are taught in Shona and he has to walk a long way to and from school.

Teacher
Mudzidzisi
Umbalisi

Student
Mudzidzi
Umfundi

Lesson
Chidzidzo
Isifundo

Homework
Basa re kumbai
Umsebenzi wangekhaya

WE HAVE THE MOST FUN IN OUR...

MUSIC LESSONS

We play these instruments:

MBIRA/THUMB PIANO

DRUM

HOSHO/RATTLE

MARIMBA

PE LESSONS
At school we play lots of different sports: soccer, rugby, cricket, netball, and athletics

DID YOU KNOW?

Soccer (football) is the most popular sport in Zimbabwe. The national men's soccer team is called 'The Warriors' and the women's team, the 'Mighty Warriors'.

LET'S PLAY

In the playground at school, one of my favourite games to play is...

KUDODA/NHODO
Equipment: a wooden or metal bowl filled with 20–30 small stones

Players: 2-3

We fill the bowl with the stones, then my friends and I sit in a circle around the bowl. Whoever goes first, picks up a stone and throws it in the air. Before the stone lands, that player tries to pick up as many other stones from the bowl as they can. Once we have all had a turn, the stones are counted and the one who has collected the most is the winner. I don't know why, but Marvelous always wins... I think he must have the biggest hands!

Play
Tamba
Ukudlala

32

LET'S LEARN

NUMBERS

I have been helping Makawa learn how to count to ten and say her alphabet. Do you want to learn with us?

1 MOTSI
KUNYE

2 PIRI
KUBILI

3 TATU
KUTHATHU

4 INA
KUNE

Learn
Dzidza
ukufunda

5 **SHANU**
KUHLANU

6 **TANHATU**
KUYISITHUPHA

7 **NOMWE**
KUYISIKHOMBISA

8 **SERE**
KUYISITSHIYANGALOMBILI

9 **PFUMBAMWE**
KUYISITSHIYANGALOLUNYE

10 **GUMI**
KULITSHUMI

THE ALPHABET

Learning the alphabet is also fun! How many can you say?

A EYI / AAH

B BHII / BAH

C SII / CAH

D DHII / DII

E I / EHH

F EFU / FF

G JII / GAH

H ECHI / HAH

I AYI / I

J JEYI / JEH

K KEYI / KAH

35

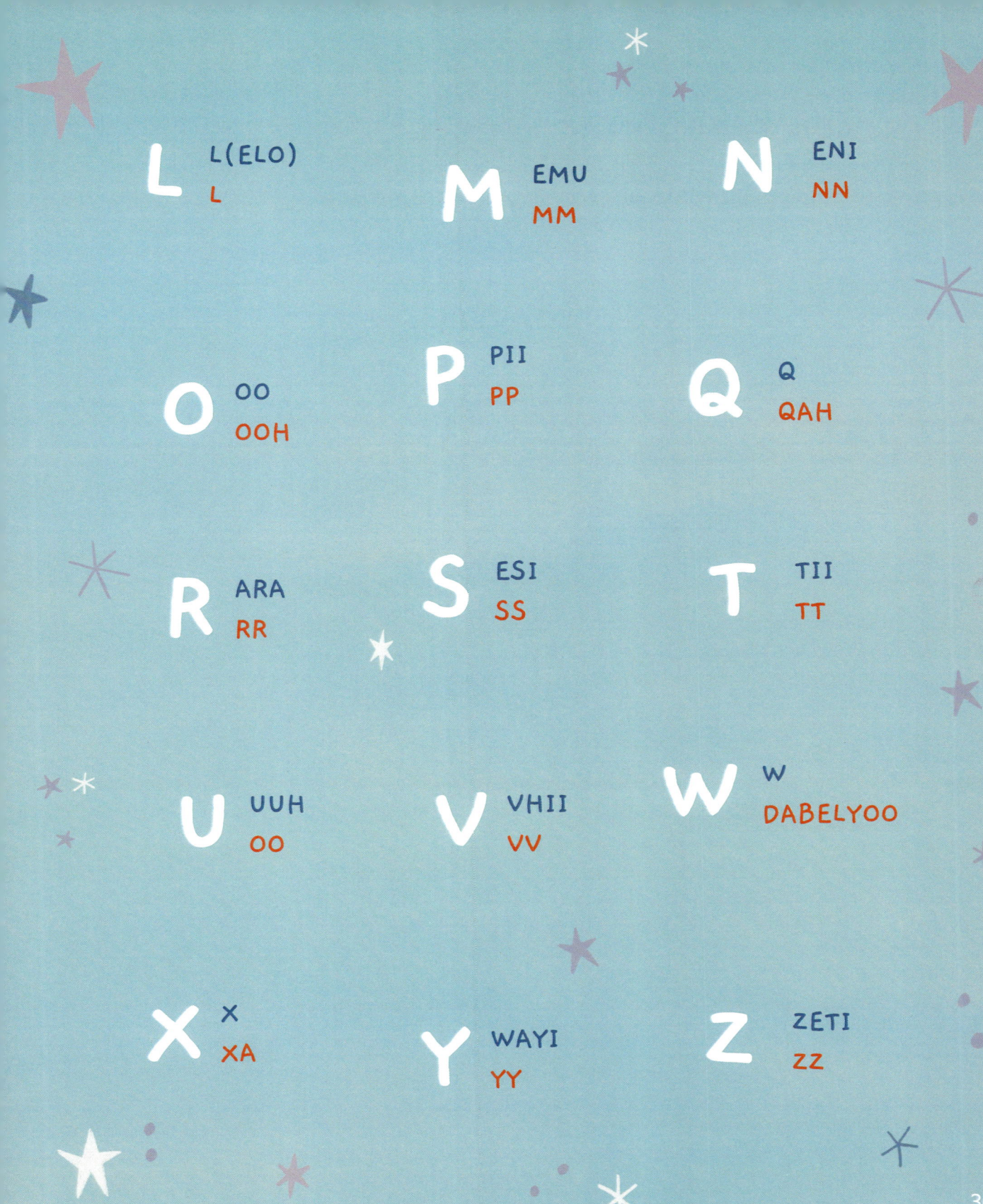

L L(ELO) / L	**M** EMU / MM	**N** ENI / NN	
O OO / OOH	**P** PII / PP	**Q** Q / QAH	
R ARA / RR	**S** ESI / SS	**T** TII / TT	
U UUH / OO	**V** VHII / VV	**W** W / DABELYOO	
X X / XA	**Y** WAYI / YY	**Z** ZETI / ZZ	

LET'S SAY

Here are some of our everyday words and phrases.
Why not try and say them?

HOW ARE YOU?
MAKADINI?
UNJANI?

HOW OLD ARE YOU?
UNE MAKORE MANGANI?
ULEMINYAKA EMINGAKI?

MY NAME IS...
ZITA RANGU NDI...
MINA NGINGU...

I AM ... YEARS OLD
NDINE MAKORE... EKUBEREKWA
NGILEMINYAKA ENGU...

GOOD MORNING
MANGWANANI AKANAKA
LIVUKILE

GOOD AFTERNOON
MASIKATI AKANAKA
LITSHONILE

GOOD NIGHT
MANHERU AKANAKA
LILALE KUHLE

I LOVE YOU
NDINOKUDA
NGIYAKUTHANDA

THANK YOU
TATENDA
NGIYABONGA

PLEASE
NDAPOTA
NGIYACELA

LET'S EAT

FOOD & DRINK

We are always really hungry in the mornings, so Amai makes us a big bowl of bota porridge made from cornmeal, peanut butter, milk, and jam.

At dinner time, Baba cooks sadza (Zimbabwe's national dish) – it is like a thick porridge made from mealie-meal (maize). We often have it with meat and a green vegetable, like spinach. He also makes my favourite – dovi, a peanut-butter stew, which we eat with the sadza. Yum!

Eat
Kudya
Ukudla

Yummy
Zvinonaka
Kumnandi

We love to snack on biltong, made from dried meat (a bit like beef jerky). We also snack on fruit. Marvelous has mango and guava trees in his garden, so his mum brings us lots of fruit. Ranga loves prickly pears, wild custard apples, and smelly berry finger leaf – he is always giggling at their names.

Sometimes Amai lets us have a sweet treat. Our favourite is mapopo candy (made from papaya). Ambuya will bake us chikenduza (candy cake) for a special treat, which is like a sweet bread-like cake covered with bright pink icing. It's delicious!

DID YOU KNOW?

Sadza is eaten using your right hand. Even if you are left-handed, it is considered rude to eat with your left hand.

LET'S CELEBRATE

We LOVE to celebrate! We do this by getting together with our family and friends. Marvelous and his family always have the best parties. We get dressed up, eat tasty food, listen to music, and dance all day long.

To Celebrate
Kupemberera   Ukujabula

Happy Birthday
Makorokoto ebhavhadhe   Suku lokuzalwa oluhle

Party
Mabiko   Emcimbini

Happy New Year
Makorokoto egore idzva

CHRISTMAS

Some years, Baba gets us a Christmas tree – other times we decorate our living room with ivy. On Christmas Eve, Ranga and I find it difficult to sleep because we get so excited. We always wake up really early on Christmas morning so we can open our presents. Then we get dressed up in our new clothes and head off to church to show our friends our new outfits. On the way home, we stop off at other people's houses along the way – eating yummy food and giving gifts. It is so much fun. When we get home, we have a big dinner of chicken and rice, and we play with our presents for the rest of the day. *We love Christmas!*

NATIONAL HOLIDAYS

We celebrate special national holidays in Zimbabwe. Sekuru says that we have these days to honour important events and people in history. We have:

21st February – Robert Mugabe's Youth Day – a day to honour the former controversial president, for his important role and influence on the country.

18th April – Independence Day – a day to celebrate our independence from the UK.

25th May – Africa Day – to celebrate and acknowledge African solidarity, unity in diversity, creativity, challenges, and successes.

2nd Monday in August – Heroes Day – to honour those who fought and died in the struggle for independence from British rule.

On national holidays, Sekuru puts the TV on so he can watch the ceremonial events. On Heroes Day, we wait quietly for them to read out the name 'Lameck Makanda'. He was our great-grandfather who is buried in Heroes Acre. Even though I don't remember him, this always makes me feel proud.

We also celebrate birthdays, Easter, Boxing Day, and New Year's Day.

GIVING GIFTS

Amai is always giving someone a gift, especially if there is a celebration going on. Our neighbours give us lots of gifts too. Sometimes they are a little boring like medicine, but other times they're fun, like a toy. Amai says no matter what the gift, we must never refuse it – that would be very rude.

DRESSING UP

Most of the time we wear the same kind of clothes that sisi Netsai and bhudi Munyaradzi wear in the UK. On special occasions, some of our family get dressed up in traditional dress – especially on holidays like Independence Day and Heroes Day. It's so fun to wear lots of bright colours, beautiful beads, and headscarves.

EATING

We often eat oxtail, chicken, beef stew, or lamb on special occasions. The bigger the occasion, the bigger the dinner, like on Christmas Day.

PLAYING MUSIC

We love music and there is always music playing on celebration days wherever we go. Even at home, when Baba is cooking breakfast before we get ready to go out, he dances around the kitchen to music and sings along. Ranga tries to copy him and pretends the pots are drums – it gets us in the party mood. Our favourite types of music are: mbube – sung by a male choir without any instruments, and chimurenga, which is played using a mbira.

DANCE

If there is music playing, everyone will be dancing. If we go to see a performance, the audience is often asked to join in and dance. Ambuya is the best dancer; she dances for hours and is always the last one dancing. She says that sometimes she and her friends have danced for days. She has been trying to teach us her favourite dances, jerusarema and the muchongoyo, which are performed to the beat of a drum.

LET'S GET LUCKY

What do you do when your tooth falls out, or what are things that bring you good luck? Here are some of ours...

TOOTH
When your tooth falls out you must throw it above your head onto a roof, or else another tooth will not grow back in its place.

HICCUPS
If someone has hiccups, you can cure them by doing something that frightens them.

SNEEZING
If someone sneezes, you say 'svikai', which is a way of asking good spirits to come.

Luck
Rombo rakanaka
Inhlanhla

GOOD LUCK

If a bird poops on you it is a sign of good luck.

The dove is a symbol of good luck.

BAD LUCK

If you are going on a journey and you see a mongoose crossing the road, it is a sign of bad luck, so you should turn back and not continue the journey.

The owl is a symbol of bad luck.

LET'S DREAM

Sometimes we close our eyes and dream about what we would like to be when we grow up.

Do you know what you would like to be?

Dream
Kurota
Ukuphupha

I WANT TO BE AN ACTRESS BUT ALSO A VOLUNTEER, BECAUSE I LOVE HELPING OTHER PEOPLE. TWO OF MY FAVOURITE ACTORS ARE:

THANDIWE NEWTON OBE
The name 'Thandiwe' means 'beloved' in Ndebele, Zulu, Xhosa, and Swati.

Thandiwe was born and raised in England to a Zimbabwean mother and an English father. I like her because she is Amai's favourite actress. Amai told me she has won lots of awards, including being invited to Buckingham Palace to receive an OBE from the Queen. This is because she is a talented actress, and she does a lot of work for charity.

DANAI GURIRA
The name Danai means 'love each other'.

Danai is an actress who plays General Okoye (my favourite character) in the film Black Panther. She is also in some of the Avengers movies, which I haven't seen yet. Danai also does a lot of very important charity work. Amai told me she helps raise awareness of female inequality and helps to provide opportunities to young actors. She is also a UN Women's Goodwill Ambassador.

My parents think I would
make a great author, like...

TSITSI DANGAREMBGA
This name means 'trouble; hardship'.

Baba tells me that Tsitsi is a novelist, playwright, and filmmaker. Her mother was, in fact, the first black woman in Southern Zimbabwe to obtain a university degree. She spent time in both England and Zimbabwe growing up. She started writing and directing plays when she discovered that there were no plays with roles for black women, so she wanted to lead the way. Tsitsi has won many awards for her film writing and directing.

Ranga is only six but he always has lots of cool ideas
and loves creating things! My parents think he will
be an inventor like...

WILLIAM SACHITI

William is a Zimbabwean-born entrepreneur and inventor. He studied robotics and AI at university and he set up his first business when he was 19. He has since created and sold many other businesses. He recently invented Kar–go, a robot-driven car that delivers packages. Ranga thinks this is cool! We saw him once on the TV show Dragons' Den.

Marvelous was named after the famous footballer, Marvelous Nakamba. He is always pretending to be him when he is playing and says his dream is to play football just like him one day...

MARVELOUS NAKAMBA

Marvelous was born in Zimbabwe. His mum worked very hard to buy him his first-ever pair of football boots. He started playing professional football when he was 16. He has played for clubs in France and Belgium, as well as for the Premier League Club, Aston Villa. He also plays for the Zimbabwean national team.

WE HOPE THAT YOU HAD FUN EXPLORING ZIMBABWE WITH US. MARVELOUS, RANGA, AND I REALLY ENJOYED SHOWING YOU AROUND. WE HOPE TO SEE YOU BACK SOON!

GOODBYE

SALA KAKUHLE
(XHOSA)

BHAIBHAI
(SHONA)

LISALE KUHLE
(NDEBELE)

SALA HANTLE
(SOUTHERN SOTHO)

National anthem
Nziyo yenyika
Ingoma yezwe

MEANING OF THE FLAG

Green	Agriculture and rural areas
Yellow	The wealth of minerals (mainly gold)
Red	The blood shed during the first and second wars (in the struggle for independence)
Black	The heritage/race/ethnicity of the black majority
White triangle	The sign of peace
The Golden Bird	Known as the 'great Zimbabwe bird', it is the national symbol of Zimbabwe.
The Red Star	The nation's aspirations

HISTORY

100,000 years ago	San hunter-gatherers made arrowheads
c 2000 years ago	Bhantu farmers settled in the region
c 1100	Kingdom of Mapungubwe and Great Zimbabwe were built
1684-1834	Rozwi Empire Nbdele
1880s	Cecil Rhodes arrives with the British South Africa Company
1923-1965	The British ruled Southern Rhodesia
1939	World War II began and many Zimbabweans were enlisted to fight in Europe
1955	Building of the Kariba Dam began
1965	Independence from the UK
1980	Robert Mugabe appointed President
2000-6	Civil unrest, food and inflation crisis
2017	Mugabe resigned after a military coup; Emmerson Mnangagwa became president

THE AUTHORS

ANNA MAKANDA

Anna was born in Gweru, Zimbabwe, and raised in London, along with her older sister. Her father is Zimbabwean and her mother, Scottish. Growing up, Anna always dreamed of owning her own business. She started her career as an accountant but soon realised it was time to pursue her dreams. That was when she set up her own fitness brand. In her spare time, you will find her spending time with family and friends, chasing after her two very energetic children, or writing a book or two!

SHARMANE BARRETT

Sharmane was born and raised in London, along with her five sisters. Her father is Jamaican and her mother, Trinidadian-English. Growing up, Sharmane was encouraged to pursue a career as a lawyer but after completing her legal studies, she soon realised that law was not for her. She began working in legal recruitment, which gave her an opportunity to live in Singapore for almost four years. Sharmane's passions are travelling and boxing – although these days there is a lot less travelling to exotic destinations, and a lot more time in the gym.

THE ILLUSTRATOR

NATÀLIA JUAN ABELLÓ

Natàlia was born in Barcelona, where she grew up with her older brother, father, and mother. She has loved drawing since she was little and was often found creating and daydreaming as a young girl. Pursuing her dream of working in a creative job, she studied to become a fashion designer but very quickly realised her real passion was to illustrate, especially children's books. Natàlia moved to the UK many years ago and now lives in a small countryside village. She loves nature, and she's happiest when taking long hikes with her partner and little doggy.

OUR GRATITUDE

We would like to say thank you and extend our gratitude to:

Everyone who helped us with the research; Anna's family, including Mum, Dad, Sister, Uncle Munyaradzi, cousin Bothwell, and friend Netsai Dandajena, for your advice, opinions, and most importantly, time. Thank you.

Our editor, Amber, who helped us make our facts engaging to our young readers; our copywriter Lisa; our proof-reader, Josie; and Martyn, our wonderful designer, who not only made our books look as beautiful as they do but also helped us articulate our vision so perfectly. To our incredibly talented illustrator, Natàlia, for bringing Tendai, Marvellous, and Ranga to life, and for showcasing the magic of Zimbabwe.

And not forgetting all our little people for helping us pick the designs and road-testing the content.

Each other. This is a passion project for us both and to be able to share this journey with a best friend is the dream.

Anna and Sharmane

OUR MISSION

Our mission is to help ignite a child's interest in their roots and empower them to become culturally confident. We aim to do this by providing parents and caregivers factual yet engaging resources to help them teach their children about their culture and heritage.

OUR SOCIAL IMPACT

Children everywhere should have access to education. This is why for every book sold we will be donating a percentage of the proceeds to the OWMR fund which aims to support charities that do exactly that.

COPYRIGHT

First published 2021
Text Copyright ©: Anna Makanda and Sharmane Barrett
Illustration Copyright ©: Natàlia Juan Abelló

Printed in the UK
ISBN: 978-1-7399365-3-2
www.ourworldmyroots.com

All rights reserved. No part of this book may be reproduced in any form by an electronic or mechanical means, including information storage and retrieval systems, without permission in writing from the publisher, except by a reviewer who may quote brief passages in a review.

This is a work of creative nonfiction. Some parts have been fictionalised in varying degrees, for various purposes.

The publishers will be pleased to make good any omissions or rectify any mistakes brought to their attention at the earliest opportunity.

A SPECIAL THANKS TO
JOSHUA MAKANDA-TANSEY,
AGED 13, FOR DRAWING THIS
ZIMBABWEAN-INSPIRED PATTERN.

OUR • WORLD • MY • ROOTS
ZIMBABWE

WRITTEN BY ANNA MAKANDA & SHARMANE BARRETT
ILLUSTRATED BY NATÀLIA JUAN ABELLÓ

OUR DEDICATIONS

In Anna's words:

To my parents, for always believing in me and encouraging me to shoot for the moon. To my mum, for teaching me that in order to know who you are, you must know where you come from. To my husband, for being my absolute rock through thick and thin. To my two beautiful children, who inspire me every day. And to my late grandfather, who died a national hero, fighting for our wonderful country.

In Sharmane's words:

To my parents and my sisters for being my biggest challengers, as well as my biggest supporters in life. To my nine amazing nieces and nephews, for being my constant reminder that I need to be a better me for all of the little eyes that are watching.